To:

Ella

From:

Glory Days

Date:

6 - 12 - 14

My First Book of
BIBLE
PROMISES

My First Book of
BIBLE
PROMISES

BARBOUR
PUBLISHING

Special thanks to Bonnie Jensen for her contribution to this project.

ISBN 978-1-62029-789-6

All scripture quotations, unless otherwise noted, are taken from the Holy Bible, New Life Version, Copyright 1969, 1976, 1978, 1983, 1986, Christian Literature International, P.O. Box 777, Canby, OR 97013. Used by permission.

Scripture quotations marked NLT are taken from the *Holy Bible*. New Living Translation copyright© 1996, 2004, 2007 by Tyndale House Foundation. Used by permission of Tyndale House Publishers, Inc. Carol Stream, Illinois 60188. All rights reserved.

Scripture quotations marked NKJV are taken from the New King James Version®. Copyright © 1982 by Thomas Nelson, Inc. Used by permission. All rights reserved.

Scripture quotations marked ICB are taken from the International Children's Bible®. Copyright © 1986, 1988, 1999 by Tommy Nelson™, a division of Thomas Nelson, Inc. Used by permission. All rights reserved.

Scripture quotations marked NIV are taken from the HOLY BIBLE, NEW INTER-NATIONAL VERSION®. NIV®. Copyright © 1973, 1978, 1984, 2011 by Biblica, Inc.™ Used by permission. All rights reserved worldwide.

Scripture quotations marked MSG are from *THE MESSAGE*. Copyright © by Eugene H. Peterson 1993, 1994, 1995, 1996, 2000, 2001, 2002. Used by permission of NavPress Publishing Group.

Cover and interior images: Shutterstock/suerz

Published by Barbour Publishing, Inc., P.O. Box 719, Uhrichsville, Ohio 44683, www.barbourbooks.com

Our mission is to publish and distribute inspirational products offering exceptional value and biblical encouragement to the masses.

Member of the
Evangelical Christian
Publishers Association

Printed in the United States of America.
United Graphics, Inc., Mattoon, IL 61938-6274; September 2013; D10004121

Contents

Using a childlike approach
to God's promises and prayer,
this book is a simple and fun way
to help your little one learn about
serving God. With kid-friendly
scriptures and illustrations that
highlight each topic, it's the
perfect way to fill young hearts
with the truth of God's Word
while teaching your child
how to live for Him every day!

Dear God,
Thank You for
Your promises.
Amen.

ANGER

I need God's help
when I'm mad.
He always makes
me feel better.

Now is the time to get rid of anger.

COLOSSIANS 3:8 NLT

A gentle answer turns away anger,
but a sharp word causes anger.

PROVERBS 15:1

Hot tempers start fights; a calm,
cool spirit keeps the peace.

PROVERBS 15:18 MSG

If you are angry, do not let it become sin. Get over your anger before the day is finished.

Smart people know how to hold their tongue.

Do not be quick in spirit to be angry.
For anger is in the heart of fools.

ECCLESIASTES 7:9

Don't hang out with angry people;
don't keep company with hotheads.
Bad temper is contagious—
don't get infected.

PROVERBS 22:24–25 MSG

He who is slow to get angry
has great understanding.

PROVERBS 14:29

Stop being angry. Turn away from fighting. Do not trouble yourself. It leads only to wrong-doing.

PSALM 37:8

God is all mercy and grace—
not quick to anger, is rich in love.

PSALM 145:8 MSG

Everyone should listen much
and speak little. He should be
slow to become angry.

Work at getting along with each
other and with God.

Don't insist on getting even;
that's not for you to do.
"I'll do the judging," says God.
"I'll take care of it."

Don't hit back.

ROMANS 12:19 MSG

Do all things without arguing and talking about how you wish you did not have to do them. . . . You are to shine as lights among the sinful people of this world.

PHILIPPIANS 2:14–15

Wise men turn away anger.

PROVERBS 29:8

He who is slow to anger is
better than the powerful.

PROVERBS 16:32

A man who hurts people tempts his
neighbor to do the same, and leads
him in a way that is not good.

PROVERBS 16:29

A dry piece of food with peace
and quiet is better than a house
full of food with fighting.

PROVERBS 17:1

Dear God,
When I get mad, please
help me to be nice.
Amen.

COURAGE

With God's help,
I can do anything!

I can do all things because Christ gives me the strength.

PHILIPPIANS 4:13

By not giving up, God's Word gives us strength and hope.

ROMANS 15:4

"Peace I leave with you. My peace I give to you. I do not give peace to you as the world gives. Do not let your hearts be troubled or afraid."

JOHN 14:27

You are my wonderful
God who gives me courage.

PSALM 3:3 ICB

Let us keep looking to Jesus.
Our faith comes from Him and He
is the One Who makes it perfect.

HEBREWS 12:2

"Come to Me, all of you who work and have heavy loads. I will give you rest."

MATTHEW 11:28

May [God] give your hearts comfort and strength to say and do every good thing.

2 THESSALONIANS 2:17

God has power over all things forever.

1 PETER 5:11

I am happy to be weak and have troubles so I can have Christ's power in me. I receive joy when I am weak. I receive joy when people talk against me and make it hard for me and try to hurt me and make trouble for me. I receive joy when all these things come to me because of Christ. For when I am weak, then I am strong.

2 CORINTHIANS 12:9–10

God. . .gives you strength.

ROMANS 15:5

We will receive [God's]
loving-kindness and have
His loving-favor to help us
whenever we need it.

HEBREWS 4:16

If we are sure [God] hears us when we ask, we can be sure He will give us what we ask for.

1 JOHN 5:15

"In the world you will have much trouble. But take hope! I have power over the world!"

JOHN 16:33

There is only one God.
He is the Father. All things are
from Him. He made us for Himself.
There is one Lord. He is Jesus
Christ. He made all things.
He keeps us alive.

1 CORINTHIANS 8:6

Dear God,
Thank You for helping
me be brave when I have to
do things that aren't easy.
Amen.

FAITH

I believe in my heart that
God will do what He says.
That's faith!

You are all children of God
through faith in Christ Jesus.

GALATIANS 3:26 NLT

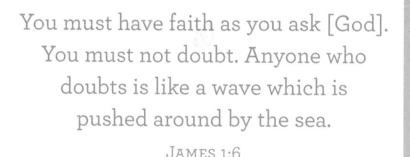

You must have faith as you ask [God].
You must not doubt. Anyone who
doubts is like a wave which is
pushed around by the sea.

JAMES 1:6

You have never seen [God] but you love Him. You cannot see Him now but you are putting your trust in Him. And you have joy so great that words cannot tell about it.

1 PETER 1:8

Now faith is being sure we will get what we hope for. It is being sure of what we cannot see.

HEBREWS 11:1

"Anything is possible if
a person believes."

MARK 9:23 NLT

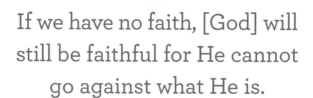

If we have no faith, [God] will
still be faithful for He cannot
go against what He is.

2 TIMOTHY 2:13

If you say with your mouth that Jesus is Lord, and believe in your heart that God raised Him from the dead, you will be saved from the punishment of sin.

ROMANS 10:9

Jesus said to him, "Thomas, because you have seen Me, you believe. Those are happy who have never seen Me and yet believe!"

JOHN 20:29

I will give thanks to the Lord with all my heart. I will tell of all the great things You have done.

PSALM 9:1

Let us come near to God
with a true heart full of faith.
Our hearts must be made clean from
guilty feelings and our bodies
washed with pure water.

HEBREWS 10:22

Get your strength from [Jesus].

COLOSSIANS 2:7

God makes all things work together
for the good of those who love Him.

ROMANS 8:28

We can trust God that He will
do what He promised.

HEBREWS 10:23

Love the Lord, all you
who belong to Him! The Lord
keeps the faithful safe.

[God] keeps His promise and
shows His loving-kindness
to those who love Him.

Be happy in the Lord.
And He will give you the
desires of your heart.

PSALM 37:4

"I have loved you just as
My Father has loved Me.
Stay in My love."

JOHN 15:9

"And you must love the Lord
your God with all your heart and
with all your soul and with
all your strength."

You have turned my crying
into dancing. You have. . .
dressed me with joy.

Dear God,
I have faith in
Your promises.
I know if You say it,
You'll do it!
Amen.

FEAR

I don't ever need to be afraid,
because God promises
to protect me and
love me—always!

When I am afraid,
I will trust in [God].

PSALM 56:3

I will not be afraid because
the Lord is with me.

PSALM 118:6 ICB

Who can keep us away from the love of Christ? Can trouble or problems?... [Nothing can] keep us away from the love of God which is ours through Christ Jesus our Lord.

ROMANS 8:35, 39

"Do not be afraid! Be strong, and see how the Lord will save you today."

EXODUS 14:13

I will not be afraid of anything,
because [God is] with me.

PSALM 23:4

"See, God saves me. I will trust
and not be afraid. For the Lord
God is my strength and song."

ISAIAH 12:2

Do not be afraid. . . . Have joy
and be glad, for the Lord
has done great things.

JOEL 2:21

"Do not fear,
for I am with you.
Do not be afraid,
for I am your God."

ISAIAH 41:10

Those who do right
do not have to be afraid.

ROMANS 13:3

You will not be afraid when
you lie down. When you lie down,
your sleep will be sweet.

PROVERBS 3:24

"Do not be afraid. I am
the First and the Last."

REVELATION 1:17

"Be strong and have strength of
heart! Do not be afraid or lose faith.
For the Lord your God is with
you anywhere you go."

JOSHUA 1:9

"Do not be afraid. You are more
important than many small birds."

MATTHEW 10:31

"I am with you to take you out
of trouble," says the Lord.

JEREMIAH 1:8

"Do not be afraid, just believe."

MARK 5:36

Do not be afraid of
those who hate you.

PHILIPPIANS 1:28

"The Lord is my Helper.
I am not afraid of anything
man can do to me."

HEBREWS 13:6

God knows how many hairs
you have on your head.
Do not be afraid.

LUKE 12:7

[God said,] "Do not be afraid. . . .
You are Mine!"

ISAIAH 43:1

Dear God,
Thank You for protecting me. Because You are always with me, I don't ever have to be afraid of anything!
Amen.

FORGIVENESS

When someone hurts my
feelings and I forgive them,
God is proud of me.
I always want to make
God happy.

"The forgiveness you give to others will be given to you."

MATTHEW 7:2 ICB

You must be kind to each other.
Think of the other person.
Forgive other people just
as God forgave you.

EPHESIANS 4:32

Forgive anyone who offends you.
Remember, the Lord forgave you,
so you must forgive others.

COLOSSIANS 3:13 NLT

"Do not fight with the
man who wants to fight."

MATTHEW 5:39

When someone does something bad to you, do not do the same thing to him. When someone talks about you, do not talk about him. Instead, pray that good will come to him. You were called to do this so you might receive good things from God.

1 PETER 3:9

"If one sinner is sorry for
his sins and turns from them,
the angels are very happy."

Luke 15:10

"If you forgive people their sins,
your Father in heaven
will forgive your sins also."

Matthew 6:14

For You are good and ready
to forgive, O Lord. You are
rich in loving-kindness to
all who call to You.

PSALM 86:5

Peter came to Jesus and said,
"Lord, how many times may my
brother sin against me and I forgive
him, up to seven times?" Jesus said
to him, "I tell you, not seven
times but seventy times seven!"

MATTHEW 18:21–22

"Forgive other people and
other people will forgive you."

LUKE 6:37

The Lord does not want any
person to be punished forever.
He wants all people to be sorry
for their sins and turn from them.

2 PETER 3:9

It will not go well for the man
who hides his sins, but he who
tells his sins and turns from
them will be given loving-pity.

PROVERBS 28:13

"But you must be sorry for your
sins and turn from them. You must
turn to God and have your sins
taken away. Then many times
your soul will receive new
strength from the Lord."

ACTS 3:19

You must be sorry for this
sin of yours and turn from it.
Pray to the Lord that
He will forgive you.

ACTS 8:22

Anyone who believes in
God's Son has eternal life.

JOHN 3:36 NLT

Anyone who belongs to Christ
has become a new person.
The old life is gone;
a new life has begun!

2 CORINTHIANS 5:17 NLT

"He washed away our sins,
giving us a new birth and new
life through the Holy Spirit."

TITUS 3:5 NLT

Become friends with God;
he's already a friend with you.
How? you ask. In Christ. God put
the wrong on him who never did
anything wrong, so we could
be put right with God.

2 CORINTHIANS 5:20–21 MSG

[God] wants all people to
be saved from the punishment
of sin. He wants them to come
to know the truth.

1 TIMOTHY 2:4

Dear God,
When someone
hurts my feelings,
I need Your help
to forgive them.
And when I make a mistake,
thank You for forgiving me!
Amen.

FRIENDSHIP

God wants me to
be a good friend.
His Word shows me how.

A friend loves at all times.

PROVERBS 17:17

"Do for other people
what you would like to
have them do for you."

LUKE 6:31

Think of other people as more
important than yourself.

A man who has friends
must be a friend.

Love never comes to an end.

1 CORINTHIANS 13:8

Let us love each other,
because love comes from God.

1 JOHN 4:7

Help each other in
troubles and problems.

GALATIANS 6:2

"You are to love each other.
You must love each
other as I have loved you."

JOHN 13:34

Do not leave your
own friend. . .alone.

PROVERBS 27:10

"Do to others whatever you would like them to do to you."

MATTHEW 7:12 NLT

"No one can have greater love than to give his life for his friends."

JOHN 15:13

If one falls down,
his friend can help him up.

ECCLESIASTES 4:10 NIV

We should do good to everyone.

GALATIANS 6:10

Dear God,
Thank You for my friends.
Help me to always
treat them just the way
I want to be treated.
Amen.

HAPPINESS

My heart is always happy
when I put my trust in God.

"Those who hear the Word of God and obey it are happy."

LUKE 11:28

Be happy in the Lord.

PSALM 37:4

If someone has the gift of showing kindness to others, he should be happy as he does it.

ROMANS 12:8

Happy is the man who
cares for the poor.

PSALM 41:1

A glad heart makes a happy face.

PROVERBS 15:13

I am made happy by [God's] Word.

PSALM 119:162

"Those who are hungry and thirsty
to be right with God are happy."

MATTHEW 5:6

Love is happy with the truth.

1 CORINTHIANS 13:6

Happy is the person
who trusts the Lord.

PSALM 40:4 ICB

"My heart is happy in the Lord."

1 SAMUEL 2:1

"Those who make peace are happy,
because they will be called
the sons of God."

MATTHEW 5:9

O taste and see that
the Lord is good.
How happy is the man
who trusts in Him!

PSALM 34:8

We are happy for the hope
we have of sharing the
shining-greatness of God.

ROMANS 5:2

For You will make those happy
who do what is right, O Lord.

PSALM 5:12

"And my spirit is happy in God."

LUKE 1:47

"Those who show loving-kindness are happy, because they will have loving-kindness shown to them."

MATTHEW 5:7

"We are more happy when we give than when we receive."

ACTS 20:35

My soul will be happy in the Lord. It will be full of joy because He saves.

PSALM 35:9

"Those who have a pure heart are happy, because they will see God."

MATTHEW 5:8

Be happy in the Lord your God.

JOEL 2:23

Happy is the nation whose God is the Lord. Happy are the people He has chosen for His own.

PSALM 33:12

Dear God,
I know I can trust
You with all my heart.
That makes me happy!
Amen.

HEAVEN

Someday I will live forever
with God in heaven.

"There is more than enough room in my Father's home. If this were not so, would I have told you that I am going to prepare a place for you? When everything is ready, I will come and get you, so that you will always be with me where I am."

JOHN 14:2–3 NLT

God is keeping careful watch
over us and the future. The Day is
coming when you'll have it all—
life healed and whole.

1 PETER 1:5 MSG

There is a crown which comes
from being right with God.
The Lord, the One Who will judge,
will give it to me on that great
day when He comes again.

2 TIMOTHY 4:8

"My sheep hear My voice and
I know them. They follow Me.
I give them life that lasts forever.
They will never be punished.
No one is able to take them
out of My hand."

JOHN 10:27–28

God's free gift is life that
lasts forever. It is given to us
by our Lord Jesus Christ.

ROMANS 6:23

Our body is like a house we live in here on earth. When it is destroyed, we know that God has another body for us in heaven. The new one will not be made by human hands as a house is made. This body will last forever.

2 CORINTHIANS 5:1

Our human bodies made from dust must be changed into a body that cannot be destroyed. Our human bodies that can die must be changed into bodies that will never die.

1 CORINTHIANS 15:53

"God will take away all
tears from their eyes."

REVELATION 7:17

We are looking for what God has
promised, which are new heavens
and a new earth. Only what is
right and good will be there.

2 PETER 3:13

If a man does things to please his
sinful old self, his soul will be lost.
If a man does things to please
the Holy Spirit, he will have
life that lasts forever.

GALATIANS 6:8

He will give eternal life to
those who keep on doing good,
seeking after the glory and honor
and immortality that God offers.

ROMANS 2:7 NLT

Jesus said. . . , "I am the One Who raises the dead and gives them life. Anyone who puts his trust in Me will live again, even if he dies. Anyone who lives and has put his trust in Me will never die. Do you believe this?"

JOHN 11:25–26

The Holy Spirit raised Jesus from the dead. If the same Holy Spirit lives in you, He will give life to your bodies in the same way.

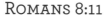

Romans 8:11

There will be no night [in heaven]. There will be no need for a light or for the sun. Because the Lord God will be their light.

Revelation 22:5

"Anyone who hears My Word and puts his trust in Him Who sent Me has life that lasts forever. He will not be guilty. He has already passed from death into life."

JOHN 5:24

We will receive the great things
that we have been promised.
They are being kept safe in heaven
for us. They are pure and will not
pass away. They will never be lost.

1 PETER 1:4

The world and all its desires
will pass away. But the man who
obeys God and does what He
wants done will live forever.

1 JOHN 2:17

Christ has gone to heaven
and is on the right side of God.
Angels and powers of heaven
are obeying Him.

1 PETER 3:22

"Why do you stand looking up into heaven? This same Jesus Who was taken from you into heaven will return in the same way you saw Him go up into heaven."

ACTS 1:11

Dear God,
Thank You for making
a home for me in heaven!
Amen.

HONESTY

God wants me to
tell the truth—always.
He never wants
me to tell a lie.

The Lord. . .delights in pure words.

PROVERBS 15:26 NLT

We want to do the right thing.
We want God and men to
know we are honest.

2 CORINTHIANS 8:21

Stand firm then,
with the belt of truth
buckled around your waist.

EPHESIANS 6:14 NIV

The Lord gives favor and honor.
He holds back nothing good
from those who walk in
the way that is right.

PSALM 84:11

The LORD. . .delights in
men who are truthful.

PROVERBS 12:22 NIV

A little earned in a right
way is better than much
earned in a wrong way.

PROVERBS 16:8

Dear children, let us not love
with words or tongue
but with actions and in truth.

1 JOHN 3:18 NIV

Good things will be given to
those who are right with God.

PROVERBS 13:21

The Lord is near to all
who call on Him, to all who
call on Him in truth.

PSALM 145:18

Love does not delight in
evil but rejoices with the truth.

1 Corinthians 13:6 niv

"Speak the truth to each other."

Zechariah 8:16 niv

I have no greater joy than
to hear that my children
are walking in the truth.

3 John 1:4 niv

"Do not lie."

LEVITICUS 19:11 NIV

For You will make those happy
who do what is right, O Lord.

PSALM 5:12

Do not do wrong to one another.

LEVITICUS 25:17

Dear God, I will be honest because I know it makes You happy! Amen.

HOPE

My hope comes from God
and His promises to me.
He has only the best
things planned for me.

Hope means we are waiting for something we do not have.

ROMANS 8:24

I will put my hope in God!

PSALM 42:11 NLT

Dear friends, we are already God's children.

1 JOHN 3:2 NLT

We know that troubles help
us learn not to give up. When we
have learned not to give up, it shows
we have stood the test. When we
have stood the test, it gives us hope.

ROMANS 5:3–4

The hope of the righteous
will be gladness.

PROVERBS 10:28 NKJV

Because Jesus was raised
from the dead, we've been given
a brand-new life and have
everything to live for,
including a future in heaven.

1 PETER 1:3 MSG

"Good will come to the man
who trusts in the Lord,
and whose hope is in the Lord."

JEREMIAH 17:7

We believe that Jesus died and then came to life again. Because we believe this, we know that God will bring to life again all those who belong to Jesus.

1 THESSALONIANS 4:14

You are my hiding place. . . .
I put my hope in Your Word.

PSALM 119:114

It's a good thing to quietly hope,
quietly hope for help from GOD.

LAMENTATIONS 3:26 MSG

I have put my hope in [God's] Word.

PSALM 119:81

This truth also gives hope
of life that lasts forever.
God promised this before the
world began. He cannot lie.

TITUS 1:2

We are of God's house if we
keep our trust in the Lord until
the end. This is our hope.

HEBREWS 3:6

We who have turned to [God]
can have great comfort knowing that
He will do what He has promised.
This hope is a safe anchor for our
souls. It will never move.

HEBREWS 6:18–19

Our hope comes from God.
May He fill you with joy and
peace because of your trust in
Him. May your hope grow stronger
by the power of the Holy Spirit.

ROMANS 15:13

I hope for Your saving power,
O Lord, and I follow Your Word.

PSALM 119:166

We speak without fear
because our trust is in Christ.

2 CORINTHIANS 3:12

I pray that you will know
about the hope given by God's call.
I pray that you will see how great
the things are that He has promised
to those who belong to Him.

EPHESIANS 1:18

I hope very much that I will have no reason to be ashamed. I hope to honor Christ with my body. . . . I want to honor Him without fear, now and always.

PHILIPPIANS 1:20

Why am I discouraged? Why is my heart so sad? I will put my hope in God! I will praise him again— my Savior and my God!

PSALM 42:11 NLT

We thank God for the hope
that is being kept for you in heaven.
You first heard about this hope
through the Good News which
is the Word of Truth.

COLOSSIANS 1:5

Now faith is being sure we
will get what we hope for. It is
being sure of what we cannot see.

HEBREWS 11:1

Dear God,
My hope is in You
and Your promises.
Thank You for being
so good to me!
Amen.

HURTS

God will always be here
for me when I'm hurt.
He will make my hurts better.

Because I suffer and am in need, let the Lord think of me. You are my help and the One Who sets me free. O my God, do not wait.

PSALM 40:17

[The Lord said,] "In this world you will have trouble. But take heart! I have overcome the world."

JOHN 16:33 NIV

The little troubles we suffer
now for a short time are making
us ready for the great things God
is going to give us forever.

2 CORINTHIANS 4:17

[Jesus said,] "Come to Me. . .
and. . .I will give you rest."

MATTHEW 11:28

We know that God makes
all things work together for the
good of those who love Him and are
chosen to be a part of His plan.

ROMANS 8:28

Even if I walk into trouble,
[God] will keep my life safe.

PSALM 138:7

Give all your worries to [God]
because He cares for you.

1 PETER 5:7

I call to God; God will help me.

PSALM 55:16 MSG

"Those who have sorrow are happy,
because they will be comforted."

MATTHEW 5:4

Is anyone among you
suffering? He should pray.

JAMES 5:13

"You are sad now. I will see you again and then your hearts will be full of joy. No one can take your joy from you."

JOHN 16:22

God is our safe place.

PSALM 46:1

[God] gives us comfort in all our troubles.

2 CORINTHIANS 1:4

Give all your cares to
the Lord and He will
give you strength.

PSALM 55:22

Our Lord Jesus Christ
and God our Father loves us.
Through His loving-favor He
gives us comfort and hope
that lasts forever.

2 THESSALONIANS 2:16

The Lord is good, a safe place in times of trouble. And He knows those who come to Him to be safe.

NAHUM 1:7

I am sure that our suffering now cannot be compared to the shining-greatness that [God] is going to give us.

ROMANS 8:18

When he falls, he will not be thrown down, because the Lord holds his hand.

PSALM 37:24

Dear God,
Thank You for coming
to my rescue when I'm hurt.
You always know just
what I need when
I'm feeling down.
Amen.

KINDNESS

God wants me to be
kind to others so they can
see His love in me.

Don't ever stop being kind. . . .
Let kindness and truth
show in all you do.

PROVERBS 3:3 ICB

"Give to any person who
asks you for something. If a person
takes something from you,
do not ask for it back."

LUKE 6:30

Each of us should live to please his neighbor. This will help him grow in faith.

ROMANS 15:2

When someone does something bad to you, do not do the same thing to him. When someone talks about you, do not talk about him. Instead, pray that good will come to him. You were called to do this so you might receive good things from God.

1 PETER 3:9

God has chosen you. You are
holy and loved by Him. Because
of this, your new life should be full
of loving-pity. You should be kind to
others and have no pride. Be gentle
and be willing to wait for others.

COLOSSIANS 3:12

"You must have loving-kindness
just as your Father
has loving-kindness."

LUKE 6:36

The Lord. . .said, "Do what is right and be kind and show loving-pity to one another. . . . Do not make sinful plans in your hearts against one another."

ZECHARIAH 7:9–10

"Love your enemies! Do good to them. . . . Then your reward from heaven will be very great, and you will truly be acting as children of [God]."

LUKE 6:35 NLT

Laugh with your happy
friends when they're happy;
share tears when they're down.

ROMANS 12:15 MSG

We should do good to everyone.
For sure, we should do good to
those who belong to Christ.

GALATIANS 6:10

Be kind to Christian
brothers and love them.

2 PETER 1:7

He who hates his neighbor sins,
but happy is he who shows
loving favor to the poor.

PROVERBS 14:21

"Give to any person who asks you for something. Do not say no to the man who wants to use something of yours."

Anyone who shows no loving-kindness will have no loving-kindness shown to him when he is told he is guilty. But if you show loving-kindness, God will show loving-kindness to you when you are told you are guilty.

JAMES 2:13

Those who follow this way will have God's peace and loving-kindness. They are the people of God.

GALATIANS 6:16

"The loving-kindness of
the Lord is given to the people
of all times who honor Him."

LUKE 1:50

"Those who show loving-kindness
are happy, because they will have
loving-kindness shown to them."

MATTHEW 5:7

Dear God,
I want to be kind,
showing Your love
to others every day!
Amen.

LONELINESS

When I feel alone,
I can talk to God.
He's always here for me.

"I am with you always."

MATTHEW 28:20

"I am with you.
No one will hurt you."

ACTS 18:10

"You will look for the Lord
your God. And you will find
Him if you look for Him with
all your heart and soul."

DEUTERONOMY 4:29

"When you pass through the waters, I will be with you."

ISAIAH 43:2

"The Lord knows those who are His."

2 TIMOTHY 2:19

"The eyes of the Lord watch over those who do right."

1 PETER 3:12 NLT

[The Lord said,] "See, I am with you. I will care for you everywhere you go."

GENESIS 28:15

I will not be afraid of anything,
because You are with me.

PSALM 23:4

God has said, "I will never
leave you or let you be alone."

HEBREWS 13:5

Then you will call, and the
Lord will answer. You will cry,
and He will say, "Here I am."

ISAIAH 58:9

"The Lord is with you when
you are with Him. If you look for
Him, He will let you find Him."

2 CHRONICLES 15:2

If you live in love,
you live by the help of
God and God lives in you.

1 JOHN 4:16

"I will be a Father to you,
and you will be my
sons and daughters,
says the Lord Almighty."

2 CORINTHIANS 6:18 NIV

[God said,] "I've called
your name. You're mine."

ISAIAH 43:1 MSG

"[God] is not far from
each one of us."

ACTS 17:27

Dear God,
I never need to feel alone.
You are always
here to make me
feel safe and special.
You love me—
Your Word tells me so!
Amen.

LOVE

God's love for me is so big,
I can't even measure it.

If God so loved us, we also
ought to love one another.

1 JOHN 4:11 NKJV

God has shown His love to us by
sending His only Son into the world.
God did this so we might have
life through Christ.

1 JOHN 4:9

"No eye has ever seen or no ear has ever heard or no mind has ever thought of the wonderful things God has made ready for those who love Him."

1 CORINTHIANS 2:9

For I know that nothing can keep us from the love of God.

ROMANS 8:38

Love each other as
Christian brothers.
Show respect for each other.

ROMANS 12:10

The love of God has come
into our hearts through the Holy
Spirit Who was given to us.

ROMANS 5:5

The Lord takes care of
all who love Him.

PSALM 145:20

God is love. If you live in
love, you live by the help of
God and God lives in you.

1 JOHN 4:16

You obey [God] when you
do this one thing, "Love your
neighbor as you love yourself."

GALATIANS 5:14

This is love! It is not that
we loved God but that He loved us.
For God sent His Son to pay for our
sins with His own blood.

1 JOHN 4:10

God has taught you
to love each other.

1 THESSALONIANS 4:9

"God so loved the world
that He gave His only Son."

JOHN 3:16

God showed His love to us.
While we were still sinners,
Christ died for us.

ROMANS 5:8

Dear friends, if God loved
us that much, then we
should love each other.

1 JOHN 4:11

We have these three:
faith and hope and love,
but the greatest of these is love.

1 CORINTHIANS 13:13

"This is what I tell you to do:
Love each other just as I have
loved you. No one can have
greater love than to give
his life for his friends."

JOHN 15:12–13

"You are to love each other.
You must love each other as
I have loved you. If you love
each other, all men will know
you are My followers."

JOHN 13:34–35

Love each other with a
kind heart and with a mind
that has no pride.

1 PETER 3:8

The Lord came to us from
far away, saying, "I have loved
you with a love that lasts forever.
So I have helped you come to
Me with loving-kindness."

JEREMIAH 31:3

"I have loved you just
as My Father has loved Me.
Stay in My love."

JOHN 15:9

" 'You must love the Lord your God with all your heart and with all your soul and with all your mind.' This is the first and greatest of the Laws. The second is like it, 'You must love your neighbor as you love yourself.' "

MATTHEW 22:37–39

Dear God,
Please help me love
others as much as
You love me!
Amen.

OBEDIENCE

Obedience is a very big word!
It means to do what God's
Word says. Doing what God
says shows just how much
I love Him.

We are taught to have nothing
to do with that which is against God.
We are to have nothing to do with
the desires of this world. We are
to be wise and to be right with God.
We are to live God-like
lives in this world.

TITUS 2:12

Those who obey what they
have been taught are happy.

PROVERBS 29:18 ICB

"Let your light shine in front of men. Then they will see the good things you do and will honor your Father Who is in heaven."

MATTHEW 5:16

God is helping you obey Him. God is doing what He wants done in you.

PHILIPPIANS 2:13

For if a man belongs to Christ,
he is a new person. The old
life is gone. New life has begun.

2 Corinthians 5:17

"The one who loves Me is the one
who has My teaching and obeys it."

John 14:21

Remember this, whatever good thing
you do, the Lord will pay you for it.

Ephesians 6:8

So give yourselves to God.
Stand against the devil and
he will run away from you.

JAMES 4:7

We will receive from Him
whatever we ask if we obey
Him and do what He wants.

1 JOHN 3:22

Children. . .obey your parents.
This is the right thing to do.

EPHESIANS 6:1

We take hold of every thought
and make it obey Christ.

2 CORINTHIANS 10:5

Do not. . .get tired of doing good.
If we do not give up, we will get what
is coming to us at the right time.

GALATIANS 6:9

You are being made more like Christ.
He is the One Who made you.

COLOSSIANS 3:10

The man who obeys God
and does what He wants
done will live forever.

1 JOHN 2:17

Have your roots planted
deep in Christ. Grow in Him.
Get your strength from Him.
Let Him make you strong in
the faith as you have been taught.

COLOSSIANS 2:7

Children, obey your parents in everything. The Lord is pleased when you do.

Colossians 3:20

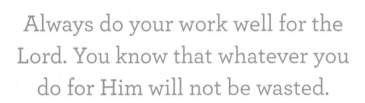

Always do your work well for the Lord. You know that whatever you do for Him will not be wasted.

1 Corinthians 15:58

Dear God,
I want to obey
Your Word every day
in everything I do.
Amen.

PATIENCE

I will be patient
and trust God—
always waiting with
a happy heart.

Patience and encouragement
come from God.

ROMANS 15:5 ICB

Rest in the Lord and be
willing to wait for Him.

PSALM 37:7

You must be willing to wait without giving up. After you have done what God wants you to do, God will give you what He promised you.

HEBREWS 10:36

Do not let yourselves get tired of doing good.

GALATIANS 6:9

God's people need to keep
true to God's Word and
stay faithful to Jesus.

REVELATION 14:12

Learn well how to wait so you
will be strong and complete
and in need of nothing.

JAMES 1:4

We are glad for our troubles also. We know that troubles help us learn not to give up. When we have learned not to give up, it shows we have stood the test. When we have stood the test, it gives us hope.

ROMANS 5:3–4

The God Who helps you
not to give up and gives you
strength will help you think
so you can please each other
as Christ Jesus did.

ROMANS 15:5

May the Lord lead your
hearts into the love of God.
May He help you as you
wait for Christ.

2 THESSALONIANS 3:5

Be willing to wait for the Lord to come again. . . . Be strong in your hearts because the Lord is coming again soon.

JAMES 5:7–8

Do not be lazy. Be like those who have faith and have not given up. They will receive what God has promised them.

HEBREWS 6:12

Do not be quick in spirit to be angry.
For anger is in the heart of fools.

ECCLESIASTES 7:9

For we belong to Christ
if we keep on trusting Him
to the end just as we
trusted Him at first.

HEBREWS 3:14

Let us hold on to the hope we say we have and not be changed. We can trust God that He will do what He promised.

HEBREWS 10:23

A man with a bad temper starts fights, but he who is slow to anger quiets fighting.

PROVERBS 15:18

It is good that one should
be quiet and wait for the saving
power of the Lord.

LAMENTATIONS 3:26

Let us keep looking to Jesus.
Our faith comes from Him and
He is the One Who makes it perfect.
He did not give up when He had
to suffer shame and die on a cross.
He knew of the joy that would
be His later. Now He is sitting
at the right side of God.

HEBREWS 12:2

But the fruit that comes from having the Holy Spirit in our lives is: love, joy, peace, not giving up, being kind, being good, having faith, being gentle, and being the boss over our own desires.

GALATIANS 5:22–23

Use the Word of God to help them do right. You must be willing to wait for people to understand what you teach as you teach them.

2 TIMOTHY 4:2

God has chosen you. You are holy and loved by Him. Because of this, your new life should be full of loving-pity. You should be kind to others and have no pride. Be gentle and be willing to wait for others.

COLOSSIANS 3:12

Dear God,
It's hard to be patient.
Please help me wait
with a smile on my face.
Amen.

PRAYER

Whenever I pray,
God is always listening.
He never goes to sleep!

Learn to pray about everything.
Give thanks to God as you
ask Him for what you need.

PHILIPPIANS 4:6

"Whatever you ask for when
you pray, have faith that you will
receive it. Then you will get it."

MARK 11:24

God's there, listening for
all who pray, for all who
pray and mean it.

PSALM 145:18 MSG

[God said,] "When you call on me, when you come and pray to me, I'll listen."

JEREMIAH 29:12 MSG

"If you get your life from Me and My Words live in you, ask whatever you want. It will be done for you."

JOHN 15:7

"When you pray, go into a room by yourself. After you have shut the door, pray to your Father Who is in secret. Then your Father Who sees in secret will reward you."

MATTHEW 6:6

"Ask, and what you are asking for will be given to you."

MATTHEW 7:7

The Lord listens
when I pray to Him.

PSALM 4:3 ICB

We are sure that if we ask
anything that [God] wants us to have,
He will hear us. If we are sure He
hears us when we ask, we can be sure
He will give us what we ask for.

1 JOHN 5:14–15

Pray for the things that are needed.
You must watch and keep on praying.
Remember to pray for all Christians.

EPHESIANS 6:18

The prayer from the heart of a man
right with God has much power.

JAMES 5:16

We will receive from Him
whatever we ask if we obey Him
and do what He wants.

1 JOHN 3:22

Let us give thanks all the
time to God through Jesus Christ.
Our gift to Him is to give thanks.

HEBREWS 13:15

"Your Father knows
what you need before
you ask Him."

MATTHEW 6:8

"Whatever you ask in My name,
I will do it so the shining-greatness
of the Father may be seen in the Son.
Yes, if you ask anything in
My name, I will do it."

JOHN 14:13–14

"All things you ask for in prayer,
you will receive if you have faith."

MATTHEW 21:22

I ask you to pray much for all men
and to give thanks for them.

1 TIMOTHY 2:1

Dear God,
I'm so glad that I
can talk to You.
You always hear my
prayers. Thank You for
loving me so much.
Amen.

SHARING

God has given me so much.
I can share with others!

[You] should give much to those
in need and be ready to share.

1 TIMOTHY 6:18

"When you have a supper,
ask poor people. Ask those who
cannot walk and those who are blind.
You will be happy if you do this.
They cannot pay you back.
You will get your pay when
the people who are right with
God are raised from the dead."

LUKE 14:13–14

"If you have two coats,
give one to him who has none.
If you have food,
you must share some."

God can give you all you need.
He will give you more than enough.
You will have everything you
need for yourselves. And you
will have enough left over to
give when there is a need.

God loves a man who gives
because he wants to give.

2 CORINTHIANS 9:7

"When you give, do not let your
left hand know what your right
hand gives. Your giving should be
in secret. Then your Father Who
sees in secret will reward you."

MATTHEW 6:3–4

"If your brother becomes poor and is not able to pay you what he owes, then you should help him as you would help a stranger or visitor."

LEVITICUS 25:35

"Be free in giving to your brother, to those in need, and to the poor in your land."

DEUTERONOMY 15:11

Happy is the man who cares for the poor. The Lord will save him in times of trouble.

PSALM 41:1

"Every man should give as he is able, as the Lord your God has given to you."

DEUTERONOMY 16:17

"Give, and it will be given to you.
You will have more than enough. . . .
The way you give to others is the
way you will receive in return."

LUKE 6:38

He who shows kindness
to a poor man gives to the Lord
and He will pay him in return
for his good act.

PROVERBS 19:17

We must remember what
the Lord Jesus said, "We are
more happy when we give
than when we receive."

Acts 20:35

God will give you enough so
you can always give to others.
Then many will give thanks to
God for sending gifts through us.

2 Corinthians 9:11

Dear God,
Help me to remember
that everything I have
is a gift from You.
Help me share these
gifts with others.
Amen.

THANKS

I will start my prayers with
a great big "Thank You" to God,
because He is so good to me.

I will give thanks to the Lord with all my heart. I will tell of all the great things You have done.

PSALM 9:1

Always give thanks for all things to God the Father in the name of our Lord Jesus Christ.

EPHESIANS 5:20

I will speak with the voice
of thanks, and tell of all
Your great works.

PSALM 26:7

Give thanks to the LORD,
for He is good!

PSALM 136:1 NKJV

"O give thanks to the Lord.
Call upon His name. Let the people
know what He has done."

1 CHRONICLES 16:8

In everything give thanks.
This is what God wants you to
do because of Christ Jesus.

1 THESSALONIANS 5:18

Do not be guilty of telling
bad stories and of foolish talk.
These things are not for you to do.
Instead, you are to give thanks
for what God has done for you.

EPHESIANS 5:4

Thank God for His great Gift.

2 CORINTHIANS 9:15

Give thanks to God in
the meetings of worship.

PSALM 68:26

I will give thanks to the Lord
because He is right and good.
I will sing praise to the name
of the Lord Most High.

PSALM 7:17

I thank Christ Jesus our Lord for the power and strength He has given me. He trusted me and gave me His work to do.

1 TIMOTHY 1:12

Give thanks to God as you ask Him for what you need.

PHILIPPIANS 4:6

Everything God made is good.
We should not put anything
aside if we can take it and
thank God for it.

1 TIMOTHY 4:4

We give thanks to You, O God.
We give thanks that Your name
is near. Men tell about the
great things You have done.

PSALM 75:1

Jesus looked up and said,
"Father, I thank You
for hearing Me."

JOHN 11:41

I always thank God when
I speak of you in my prayers.

PHILEMON 1:4

Let us honor and thank the God and Father of our Lord Jesus Christ. He has already given us a taste of what heaven is like.

EPHESIANS 1:3

Let the peace of Christ
have power over your hearts.
You were chosen as a part of
His body. Always be thankful.

COLOSSIANS 3:15

Your life should be full
of thanks to [God].

COLOSSIANS 2:7

Let us thank the God and
Father of our Lord Jesus Christ.
It was through His loving-kindness
that we were born again to a new
life and have a hope that never dies.
This hope is ours because Jesus
was raised from the dead.

1 PETER 1:3

Dear God,
Thank You for all the
good things You give me.
I love You, God!
Amen.

WORRY

Even when I'm not in control of things that happen, God doesn't want me to worry—He wants me to let Him take care of everything.

"I tell you this: Do not worry about your life. Do not worry about what you are going to eat and drink. Do not worry about what you are going to wear. Is not life more important than food? Is not the body more important than clothes?"

MATTHEW 6:25

Do not worry. Learn to pray about everything. Give thanks to God as you ask Him for what you need.

PHILIPPIANS 4:6

"Which of you can make
himself a little taller by worrying?
Why should you worry about
clothes? Think how the flowers grow.
They do not work or make cloth.
But I tell you that Solomon in all
his greatness was not dressed as
well as one of these flowers."

MATTHEW 6:27–29

I know that nothing can
keep us from the love of God.

ROMANS 8:38

God will give you everything
you need because of His great
riches in Christ Jesus.

PHILIPPIANS 4:19

"Do not worry about tomorrow.
Tomorrow will have its own worries.
The troubles we have in a day
are enough for one day."

Matthew 6:34

You have turned my crying
into dancing. . . . So my soul may
sing praise to You, and not be quiet.
O Lord my God, I will give
thanks to You forever.

Psalm 30:11–12

Thanks be to the Lord, Who carries our heavy loads day by day. He is the God Who saves us.

PSALM 68:19

The peace of God is much greater than the human mind can understand. This peace will keep your hearts and minds through Christ Jesus.

PHILIPPIANS 4:7

It is good to give thanks to
the Lord, and sing praises to
Your name, O Most High.
It is good to tell of Your loving-
kindness in the morning, and of
how faithful You are at night.

<small>PSALM 92:1–2</small>

God did not keep His own
Son for Himself but gave Him
for us all. Then with His Son,
will He not give us all things?

ROMANS 8:32

There is no wisdom and no
understanding and no words that
can stand against the Lord.

PROVERBS 21:30

God is faithful. He will not allow you to be tempted more than you can take. But when you are tempted, He will make a way for you to keep from falling into sin.

1 CORINTHIANS 10:13

"Peace I leave with you.
My peace I give to you. I do not
give peace to you as the world gives.
Do not let your hearts be
troubled or afraid."

JOHN 14:27

If you follow Christ. . .
God will be happy with you.
Men will think well of you also.
Work for the things that make
peace and help each other
become stronger Christians.

ROMANS 14:18–19

Dear God,
Thank You for taking
my worries away.
Amen.

PRAYERS
FOR LITTLE
HEARTS

God's Love

Dear Jesus, thank You for
filling my heart with Your love.
I love You. Amen.

God, I know You command us to
love everyone, but it's hard to love
the people I don't like! Help me to
see these people with Your eyes and
love them with Your heart. Amen.

Thank You, Lord, for today. I want
to make the most of it by showing
someone Your love. Amen.

Heavenly Father, thank You
for showing me You love me in
great big ways and in tiny
little details, too. Amen.

God, I'm thankful that
Your love is big enough for
the whole world. Amen.

Dear God, thank You for helping
and comforting me through the
times that I need it. Amen.

God's Word

Jesus, help me learn Your
Word so I can hide it in my heart.
When I think of a Bible verse,
it reminds me that You're here,
even though I can't see You.
Amen.

God, sometimes I'm afraid of
the dark. Mom says the Bible
is a light for me, so could You
make it light in my heart,
even if it's dark around me?
Amen.

Dear God, when things are confusing, please help me to remember to go to Your Word to find the real truth. Amen.

My Choices

God, thank You for helping me know what to do. Help me to remember to ask You for help. Amen.

Thank You, God, that You give me the strength to do anything for You. Amen.

Jesus, please forgive me for
not doing things Your way today.
Make me strong so I will make the
right decision next time. Amen.

Lord, the world is so exciting.
It's so full of things to see and do
and learn. Some of them are good
and some are not. Help me to make
choices that will honor You and
not take away from You. Amen.

My Faith

Dear Jesus, some of my friends
think believing in You is silly.
Help me be strong and honest
about how I feel about You. Amen.

Jesus, I know You choose people
to do special things for You,
but I don't feel special. I know
You can use me to do great things.
Here I am. I'm Yours. Amen.

I don't understand Your ways, God, and my heart doesn't always believe what I know in my head— that You are always doing good. Help me trust You more. Amen.

My Family

Jesus, thank You for my mom. Help me find special ways to let her know that I appreciate her. Amen.

Dear Jesus, thank You for
my dad. He's great! Amen.

God, help me to honor
my parents. Amen.

Dear Lord, please help my family
come to know You better. Amen.

God, thank You for my grandparents
and aunts and uncles and cousins.
They are special to me. Amen.

My Friends

Jesus, help me to see when my friends are hurt or sad so I can share Your love with them. Amen.

Jesus, I want You to use me to tell my friends about You. Please show me opportunities to do that. Amen.

Lord, help me to be a good friend. Help me to treat people fairly and honestly. Help me to show love, even when the other person hurts my feelings. Amen.

My Needs

Jesus, if You were able to feed more than five thousand people with just five loaves of bread and two fish, I know You can meet all my needs. Help me to trust You to take care of me. Amen.

Father God, thank You for giving me everything I need. You are so good to me. Amen.

Prayer of Salvation

Dear God, thank You for sending Your Son to die on the cross for my sins. Please forgive me for all of my sins and come into my heart. I want to follow You for the rest of my life and look forward to living forever in heaven with You. Amen.

Thank You, Jesus!

Father, thank You that even though my words don't always come out right when I pray, You know what my heart means. Sometimes people misunderstand me, but You never do. I'm glad! Amen.